BACKLASH
PRESS

A pioneering publishing house dedicated to creating intelligent, vivid books. Established to inform, educate, entertain and provoke.

A Backlash Press Book
First published 2018

www.backlashpress.com

SCB Distributors
15608 South New Century Drive
Gardena, CA 90248, USA

Book designer: The Scrutineer, Rachael Adams.

Printed and bound by Ingram.

ISBN: 978-0-9955999-4-9

American Dangerous

Renée Olander

Acknowledgements

Many thanks to Finishing Line Press for publishing *A Few Spells*, and to Black Bird Press for publishing *Wild Flights*, chapbooks in which some of these poems appeared. Thanks also to these journals, anthologies, blogs and radio/podcasts in which some of these poems have appeared:

Amelia Magazine, California Quarterly, Controlled Burn, Forgotten Women, Free State Review, Frisk Magazine, Hawai'i Pacific Review: Best of the Decade 1997-2007, Heart (human equity through art) and *Heart Online, Oberon, Out of Line, Rhino, Satori, Sistersong: Women Across Cultures, Snake-Nation-Review, The Café Review, The Chronicle of Higher Education Poetry Month Blog, South Loop Review, Verse and Universe: Poems About Science and Mathematics*, and *Writers Block – WHRV 89.5 FM*

Also, my heartfelt gratitude towards Carolyn Hodgson Meyers Rhodes, who kept the faith.

Contents

who in the hell set things up
like this

— from "Poem About My Rights" by June Jordan

Scared of Devils

I was in second grade, Annie was in fifth,

When Mama opened the furnace closet door

To show us the five brown lunch bags

Lined up like on the kitchen counter

Mornings before school, a name

Penned on each in Mama's script.

I'd already seen those bags, since I,

Scared of devils, daily checked that rattling chamber—

Staples clamped the bag necks tight

So I couldn't see inside,

But I felt the hefty, hidden lumps—

Jewelry Mama portioned for each child.

What we knew of Vietnam was Dad

Went there on his ship and came home

Every nine months with jewelry:

Long strands of creamy and blue-black

Pearls, and pyramid stacks on platinum

Of sapphires, opals, rubies, jade.

Nights, through walls, we heard low tones,

Muffled rumblings when Dad was home.

Mama kept to the house, mending bruises

Well after he went back to sea.

If anything ever happens to me,

Mama warned and eyed the bags,

Make sure you kids get these.

Mary Quite Contrary Explains:

"A helicopter overhead hammers its blades: my whole life

I've lived near enough to bases to hear
Comings and goings of warplanes: took childhood trips

To warships: crawled up metal ladders, down passageways,
Inspected inner cavities where guns, engines, amphibian

Tractors hid, huge-wheeled, strange car-boats Marines
Guarded and polished. They saluted Dad.

                                                    Back then,
Mom joined Officers' Wives and Garden Club: she sewed
Our clothes, canned peaches, crabapple, strawberry jam:

She kneeled to plant bulbs before she died: she nursed
The yard like a child's grave: roses, pansies, scattered oaks,

Magnolias, willows, rows of red and yellow tulips,

Multicolored clusters of irises: she cut flowers for tables,

Fed many.

Now Dad's got strategic defense wired in

At home, his neighbors tucked into *Chemlawns*: he

Says he can't believe he's *grown to hate Puerto Ricans*:

The hometown he retired to *Taken over*, he says, not like when

He was a kid: he yarns on about afternoon Westerns:

Tickets for a nickel and popcorn just a penny! He watches

Rambo reruns with grandsons: animated soldiers sing

Don't you change that channel, Son! Swinging guns

Between commercials and cartoons: it's in HD, and

Maybe that's why I dreamt that tax dollar death squads

Shattered my bedroom glass: ambushed my middle class

Imagination: last night: plaster masks tossed cash from floats

Full of pulp, brains bashed by cops, bombs, or shrapnel

Hitting home: white America for once:

What would you dream

If your brother joined *Militia of Montana*? Clenched his jaw and spat

Because *blacks showed up* at Mom's funeral?

They goddam won't be at mine! He said, like

We'd have to turn black folks away. Of Mom's estate,

Daughters got silver services, china, pearls, and gold chains:

Guess who got Grandpa's guns? Mom willed them to the son

Who hardly makes rent on top of munitions: Dad sends cash

To atone when he can: claims to wake ashamed every day

For conduct unbecoming, menace in the blood he handed down:

In my garden, I grieve, mostly talk to dirt and weeds."

Song for a Ghost of Lake Drummond

The landfill edges up against peat bog

And magnetic hot-spot—the so-called Great

Dismal Swamp, where snakes

Still dangle from limbs along the shallow

Crooked canal George Washington dug,

His compass tricked off-track. Here

Black bears keep house

And a mercury-looking lake

Laps shores where shells

Tell ocean tales, and one can slip

In to skim some heat off summer.

Bald cypress knees and trunks

Rise like knobby wisdom.

According to legend,

A native spirit lights her lamp

And roams some nights

Looking under the moon for her love.

A dark cusp of landfill liner

Doesn't deter her. Wide-mouthed

Moccasins glide among cypress,

Bits of tackle and cloth, crackling plastic.

She doesn't find what she seeks.

She never does.

And the prehistoric lake lives

On high ground

Not far from where sludge

Sucks amber sap and spits

Certain alchemies back,

Along shrunken edges of refuge,

Lush as composted death.

When shadows fade into morning

Motors, bug sprays, sodas,

Floating lures and rubber boots,

Not much marks her passage.

What It Was

So we were at my place.

I was young. So was he.

It was evening, I was tired.

So was he. And very drunk.

When I offered to call a cab

He said, *O No*

I'm not leaving till you give.

We had been all day in the city—

Museums, lunch, cocktails.

Christian slurred his words

And walked funny

By early evening.

He was handsome when he wasn't drunk.

The first time I saw him

I thought of a Greek god.

What? I said.

You know, he said,

You know you want it.

What? I said,

Embarrassed for him, such a fool.

I said, *you're drunk, Christian.*

He said, *you want it Baby.*

I said, *No,* but he said

I'm not leaving till you give.

You might not call it rape.

You probably wouldn't—

What happened, how I gave

Without a word and did not

Look at him, his pale skin.

He called his own cab.

The next day I crouched

In the shower for hours.

I called my sister.

She didn't want to hear.

She said Christian was an old friend.

I should keep it to myself.

Conquest: Turtle Island

1. On the Bay this morning

Not far from beach bathers

Who mostly gave it wide berth,

A dead turtle washed up,

Like a whole sordid decade,

A gelled and whitened blob,

Sand-crusted, half-eaten,

And faintly stinking.

A few gawkers pressed near

As if it were a circus, before

Six men in blue marine

Science uniforms

Hauled it off for study.

2. Another woman's body on the beach

Waterlogged—

Someone stumbled on her—

A whole body, not a headless torso

Like one a dump truck driver

Spotted last week, spilling from a trash heap,

No sign of her legs or hands.

After the news I dreamt my hands

Were cut off, and the train I rode

Barreled through industrial

Bowels of seaboard cities.

Sunset near the edge of town,

A streak comes down through clouds

And lights a mound of landfill.

Adult Female, in Her Own Home

Evenings, exhausted, I push through the door,

Close and chain it, then go scrub

Workweek soot off my skin,

Still fairly youthful-looking,

Though I don't get many hoots anymore.

I've read one woman in every four

Or ten or twelve

Will be raped, and I

Am one. I wear

No makeup. I fork

My keys between my knuckles

From my car to my front door. Inside

I wash my face with grains of sand

To clean my pores of living

Near cars and coal piers. Dirt

Comes in the cracks.

And I hide weapons in every room:

Crystal candlesticks beside my bed

Are meant for bashing. I go

To sleep with my eyes wide open,

And in my dreams I time myself

Grabbing various kitchen knives.

Power-Walking in Colonial Place

(A Virginia Neighborhood)

The way gouged trees grow around wires,

Cup them like chalices against cloud grays,

Works for squirrels, who leap and chirp,

Seeming nutty half the time, like Hope

With her teller-booth chat, counting cash

Amid *how-you-dos*. Who can help

Feeling queasy looking up—what

Grace these branches reach for, despite

Their centers pruned for currents?

They don't wheeze. I breathe evenly

Through the nose. Ground-level ozone

Could be worse! Grandfather's refrain

In a children's book. Good to get out

And watch sun set over the neighborhood river

Of revolutionary fame – *Lafayette* –

And consider how Columbus grew bitter

As his century waned, lamenting how

At destruction, everyone's adept. Islands

He thought he named, spoiled after all.

Everything near and far—the perennial

Flowers people are, generations pursuing,

And how land heals, battlefields groomed

Into parks with markers that don't fester.

Earth absorbs blood, no worse for it.

I wish for a bit of bottled water, remember

After the circus, the kids asked whether

Lions know there's meat in us. Fresh

Coffee when I get home, on with the day,

Barely a care about who picked my beans,

Scarcely any nostalgia for frogs,

Who, weirdly humanlike,

Once proliferated all over,

Got stupidly squashed in gutters and streets –

Who mourns their die-offs and deformities?

I'm guessing insects benefit.

I swat at whatever flutters near

My broken bathroom nightlight, cracked

"Joy" in red stained-glass letters and holly

Leaves I glued back together. Sky's

Quick to shift—pinks and blues –

Dramatic, passing, certain

As frogs and trees. How not to be

Complicit? I head home aerobically fit.

Seasons keep their secrets—exposed, quiet

Rings in severed trunks piled roadside.

Llewellyn Avenue Redevelopment

The lame parade along Llewellyn Avenue:

A stiff limper, an old dude or gentleman,

A woman whose foot spills out of her shoe,

A hag whose ankle sags over her shoe,

And collections of bundles carried by men

Made lame but parading Llewellyn Avenue.

Traipsing or dragging down Llewellyn Avenue,

These huddled masses bring no sense of Zen

To homeowners with housekeepers and good shoes

Who use their money and power to choose

To get rid of park benches homeless men

Sat on to make the park a refuge.

Tree-lined, flood prone Llewellyn Avenue,

Once in decline, known for drug busts and dens,

Gentrified, and now sports high-end shoes.

Norfolk removing park benches was news:

No rest for the shiftless downtrodden.

Rush hour blows fast down Llewellyn Avenue.

The trudging lame could use some new shoes.

Walking Around, Trying to Breathe

(after Neruda and Seibles)

It so happens I've grown sick of being white,

Notwithstanding the luxury of saying so,

The luxury of waltzing through Customs without a glance,

Despite the weed in my bag. Like I can do no harm.

I'd like to be a black man in a Rasta hat

Selling pipes at the market on St. Thomas—

San Tómas Columbus named it,

As if he were Adam.

To cast off the bone-white script,

To sigh free of the weight of my white-woman skin,

The myth of me. As if I weren't a hoochie-mama

At heart, connected to the earthen dark

Of love in beds of all sorts, the ripe garden.

It happens that I'm sick and tired of whiteness—

The threat of me on the street anywhere

When black women see me with a brother

They think I stole. As if I were Scarlet O'Hara

Keeping him to plow my fertile fields.

Like I'm a trap. Or a turncoat to *the white race*

White men who pass me say with stares—

The *evil stare*, an ebony lover called it

In rural Virginia, where we watched our backs.

I'm sick of white men thinking that I'm their birthright,

That I would want them if a black buck

Hadn't fucked me first, and my father

Telling my sister, *you know it isn't true -*

What they say about black men -

Wondering whether my love is jungle fever.

I'd like to dip my skin in turquoise,

Magenta, or periwinkle blue—to lose the paleface

The world has learned to hate. To look

Less like the women who packed picnics

For lynch mobs, hands that rocked

So many hooded cradles.

Too dark to get invited to the country club.

It happens I've grown tired

Of white privilege, the system,

The homogenizing machine.

I'm sick of my skin seeming to agree

That progress came from genocide,

That white women wearing gold and diamonds

Aren't blood-splattered, like conquistadors.

I'm sick of looking standard, entitled—

When what I wish for

Is a voodoo revolution, some mojo, skin salve, a spell—

Whatever might heal history, the white stain.

Chapultepec, the Motherland

Tlaquepaque, México

Little grasshopper woman cross-legged on the sidewalk

Outside the stucco shop in Tlaquepaque,

Have you got the tourists cornered, or have they got you?

Miniature grasshopper woman with a baby in the cradle

Of your legs on the dry ground of grasshoppers,

Do you ever think of your country's flag,

The *rojo, blanco, verde*— while your fingers work a sap

To glue love beads into sacred signs: scorpion, deer,

The sun, peyote? We gringos tower over your blanket

And appraise your bright boxes, your frames, your earthen face

Cracked as mesa, your toothless smile blessing us and

Whatever your toddler says, something older than Spanish.

If I could speak your languages, I might ask to which

Of the one-hundred sixty groups the *rojo* represents

You belong, and what you think of the *blanco*

For Catholicism, a religion I abandoned long ago

But carry guilt from—dizzy in the heat, I consider

The history of México, *Chapultepec*, Land of Grasshoppers,

Where *verde* stands for independence. My guide

Bargains for me: *She wants it what's your best*

Price? And I buy, spend a little more than I meant.

The Bind

The worst could have been in ancient dynasty China, where the fold

Of the foot down the middle and the curbing of the toes formed a point,

A formal shape like a bird's beak, nothing to walk on, unstable foundation

From which to run from any assailant. Can't run on a beak.

Can't run on a foot cracked down the middle, a crippled fledgling,

The point of course to raise a girl who can't run, a sitting duck,

For whatever violation and pleasure the men devised. Or maybe

The worst is African clitoris snipping, genital mutilation, the slashing

Away any possibility of pleasure, and knowledge, with dull, dirty blades.

Or maybe the worst is gender selection, as in Calcutta and Mumbai,

Preventing and perpetuating the tragic lives of girls, acid attacks, gang

Rapes, and quiet desperation. Perhaps crueler are the Saudis: anyone

"Raped" must muster so many male witnesses. Or maybe the North

American examples are more awful, the one-in-four or one-in-five, daily

News streams of crimes normalized, like tiny feet bound, babies drowned.

On First Looking, and Looking Again

(*after Keats'* "On First Looking in to Chapman's Homer")

Or like stout Cortez, when with his eagle eyes—

Who knew what worlds would fall from what he saw?

Or how the prism-shifts of enterprise

Would sparkle round the global market's maw?

But after all, had Keats first checked his facts,

He would have known Balboa, not Cortez,

First sighted that vast sea—he might have asked

More of what conquest meant, and history says.

Yet, when I first read young Keats' poem of awe

He swept me into imagined realms of gold

And neither did I question what I saw

Or surmised. An exercise of privilege very old.

Legend has it friends told Keats of his mistake

And he preferred to err for beauty's sake.

Recounting Languages We Spoke

(an adulterated sonnet)

He said that when he said he loved he meant

Just then, that moment. *Love lies in the heat*

He said, *You know what I mean?* And I thought

Something abiding lingered in the word—

Silly me. So no wonder he forgot

After kisses cooled what his lips had let

Slip; dissolved words require no dumb regret

As memory might. Absurd to say he lured

Me into love. Better to blame the blurred

Power of words. *And so I should have spent*

My love at once? I asked in sound defeat,

Carpe diem, sweet nothings, don't repent?

His eyes responded with such cool reserve

I wondered what I'd thought I could preserve.

Desdemona, Smothered

This man who sang encomia to me,

Who gave me to think he thought me highest

Among women, and invoked deities—

Diana, the demigoddess Muses—

That he of all men should seek to hurt me

Seemed wholly inconceivable, a joke,

Thus when loyal Emilia warned me

Of fickleness in men, their depravity,

Her meaning was a distant foreign country:

Then into our bedchamber that last night

Othello's warlike posture and dark eyes

Matched his monstrous words of blame and fright

And murdered me, his loss of faith was death—

Before that pillow caught my breath.

Down the Road from the Wedding

A billboard on the highway said

"Wife and Dog Missing – Reward for Dog."

There hung a snapshot smile.

A steeple dressed up in her veil,

Borrowed pearls and blue garter,

Elastic pulled too tight around her thigh.

A cummerbund husband cut the grass

After he smothered his better half,

Stuffed her in a garden bed.

A ring around a rosy,

A trellis and a grave –

Grown into stench of rotten buds.

A woman lost her plea before a judge

After she murdered the trousers

With kitchen ammunition.

A collar asked, "Who gives this bride?"

A groom thought flowers needed mowing.

A broom made soup of insecticide.

Gavels, spades, and stripped-down screws:

What helpful household supplies

Could balance the tilt?

A dog got hit, died in a ditch.

Drunk guests at a gala reception,

Fat flies buzz above the guts.

Till the Garbage Truck Comes

I'm glad my downstairs neighbors moved.

Their three cats tore into my trash

while the scrawny, mop-headed man with the large

Adam's apple called his unnaturally thin

sunken-eyed wife a fucking bitch, beat her

with fists and with some other object

he used once to break her leg—that night

her gut-wrenched screams to him to take her

to the hospital made me call

the police, who stopped by.

I could see him in some sweaty T-shirt open

the door, present his bloody beaten

wife to the authority, as he'd done before—

I could hear clear through the floor—

she said she fell down the stairs

with a glass in her hand.

The next morning, her leg in a cast,

she sat out on the stoop, stroking the cats.

They bought a house on the edge of town,

she three months pregnant,

sunken-eyed—her third try

at full term.

She Got the Baby

She got the baby she always wanted,

She got the ring, the baby carriage,

She got the chubby hubby-do,

She got the baby makes three.

Any baby can be a crybaby,

Any hubby can be a grump,

Any cradle needs some rocking,

Anybody can learn to dust.

Who got the doggone drunken daddy?

Who got the house without a book?

Who got the scarecrow weepy mommy?

Who got the stocking filled with soot?

The swing-set needs to be torn down,

The bicycle spokes are broken,

The toy-box is a hope chest,

The doll left one eye open.

Who doesn't want to be a grandma?

Who doesn't want a sweet reward?

Who doesn't always want a baby?

Who doesn't knock upon that door?

Any baby could be a crybaby,

Any hubby might be a drunk,

Any cradle could need rocking,

Anybody might gather dust.

Fatherly Love

Kicked out of his childless, crumbling

Second marriage, he shows up

On my doorstep, shoulders

Rounder than I recall, his chest

A nest of gray hair. He says

He's sorry and I shrug. We speak

Of love and love

Lost. He has a few drinks and is ready

To leave. I insist on fixing him

Food for the long

Drive. Half-sober, he

Watches me squint-eyed,

Picks at the dead

White flesh around his fingernails.

"Now I know," he says finally, "all

Those times I chewed you out and you

Glared at me, you were thinking, 'Look,

Bastard, someday

I'll be packing your lunch.'" He

Uproars a laugh. I half-

Smile, sting

And ache, like years ago when he cracked

A bat and the ball hit

Hard on the side of my face.

Bird's Eye View of the Environs of the Elizabeth River from My Divorced Dad's Bachelor Pad

On a balcony well above tree-line,

Listen, a saxophone spiels from a living room,

And outside – engines, jackhammers, workweek noise.

Radio towers and ventilation buildings

Flank banks of a river named for a queen.

In a crouching haze

Tugboats push gray gravel humps

And barges of coal.

Container ships and shipping yards

Help rank this river

Among the world's top-most polluted,

Still this stretch dazzles:

Glints of warship gray and oil-black flash

And above, the airspace buzzes –

Nightingale's blades lifting off to rescue

Some wounded somewhere – that complex

Of hospital buildings sits on old Mill Town,

Land filled for factories, turn of the century –

A few old warehouses still stand,

And beyond them, Navy destroyer piers

And state-of-the-art submarines –

In the other direction, the bank and railroad towers,

A world trade center where workers

Found seven layers of civilization,

Pouring foundation – Consider

The silent sponge of the wetlands –

No telling who-all trod here,

Or how to figure the night herons' opinions –

How they knew to return

A few years ago, safe

From DDT in the river. Now

Pairs of dark feathered guests

Nest in the park's tallest trees –

And over bridges, under tunnels,

Cataract-like water hosts

Thousands of cargo and leisure boats,

And folks in the neighborhood near

The chemical plant fish and crab

Despite the *No Fishing No Crabbing* signs.

Festivals at the harbor draw

Samplings of America, where slaves

Once shuffled shackled between masters

And panicked citizens hustled North

When Yellow Fever struck. But

I almost forgot why I stopped by:

To water the houseplants and swim

In the pool on the top floor where

I'll fly awhile – cool

Chlorinated blue will lick my skin,

Lift my limbs – I'll be a pale

Spirit breast-stroking, frog-kicking

Free as passion, jazz in brass and the wet

Whirls will kiss my cupping palms.

Sarah's Rites and Reflections

I didn't choose, didn't

Choose this, to be named

For my old mother's sister, dead

When she was sixteen, in starched

Victorian linen.

That Sarah was born in 1910

When her mother was already blessed

With eight sons and two

Daughters. The eldest, Mother,

Cared for Sarah,

Sickly from birth, as none of the others

Had been, pale and graceful, dull brown hair

Mother dressed with ribbons.

I was frizz-haired and freckle-faced,

A child made to parade

The name of the dead, the favorite

Dead. But still, now, at 48,

I get this way twice a year—on the birth

And death dates of my oldest son, I call

Each of my five living children, ask them

Do you know what day this is? None

Was alive when it happened, my first birth

And death. After all

These years, expecting my calls—

Like my old Mother's calls for Sarah—

They say, practically,

Oh, Mom, cut that out,

You've got five kids who love you, why

Sorrow for a son who lived three days

And would have been a vegetable?

The Apparatus of the Dark

(Notes to myself on longevity

after a lightning storm at the beach)

1. *You can touch,* Mama said.

She placed my palm on her stretched skin,

She pulled my head close so I heard

A child

    I squelched my urge to recoil from ripe

Motion there in my mother. I searched for the door

She said doctors would open.

Afterward, after prayers with her,

I lay in the night

Straining

For a sense of origin, a point

Like a faraway star I came from.

2. Imagine atoms

And clusters of cells

Driven to grow like banks of clouds.

3. My mother conceived seven lives:

Five survived, one miscarried, one died

A few hours after birth—

Mama buried a life alone

And Dad sailed home from Korea.

Next I slid

Premature,

Twice declared dead,

Packed in ice,

Till I shrieked my lungs alive.

4. Mama's body burned.

Her ashes went to sea.

Our last touch, my lips

Brushed her forehead,

Cool as shaded clay.

5. This evening I went out for broken silver

Beyond sailing scuds at dusk

And high tide. Bitter air came from somewhere

Something

Tossed up inadvertent.

Soon I'll burrow in bed and seek

Childhood dreams where palm fronds seemed

God's fingers touching down.

I'll study markings: *sacred – scared –*

How moon rims dip past sight.

Wild Flights

In Hawai'i   a palm tree was the hand of God

before I knew it as a palm shadow waving against

the window shade and even after

I knew   I felt I watched God wave

From darkness outside Honolulu's Navy housing.

Nights   after Acts of Contrition

I watched the hand   and listened

for devils under the bed

I bargained with small selves

half-lived   half-dreamt   some flights—

Like characters I learned in church   and on T.V.

I hoped to reach   the edge of the island

maybe   circle the world—

I wanted to learn whether for sure

life went on   half the planet lit   indifferent

to the trappings of my life—

bunk beds, monkey bars, branches of climbing trees—I

had notions I'd solve puzzles

of ubiquity   eternity   and other

words I didn't know.

Once in a while fear gripped   me

a devil had actually heard

and I'd whisper   Hail Maries,

watch for signs from the swaying palm.

Once I woke so sure I'd flown I tried

to prove it to my sister   who made fun

when of course I tumbled clumsy into red ant mounds

in the yard beyond the lanai:

even then I wouldn't say I couldn't fly—

I fly: I get high

when I read   touch   make love

when I close my eyes   when I inhale

music, myrrh   a smoking weed

wind's breath and flesh   merging   wholly

into all   atom-like   and taste buds delicious

like the rise of a falling bird

who finds   her wings   in time.

Sestina: To My Sisters

Can you believe I broke Mom's dresser mirror?

It sprawls like a shattered web across the floor—

All over the hardwood and wool rug beside the bed—

When it crashed I had to leave the room to breathe—

It's such a mess, I'll need patience and time

To pick it up, consider my luck.

I don't remember what turn of luck

Caused me to be the one who got the mirror.

I must've been hanging around some time

When Mom got a rage to clean—the floors

And walls so cluttered, we could hardly breathe

Till she gave away furniture, dumped their bed.

Each of us, of course, was conceived on that bed.

Signs of their passions, strokes of luck—

Maybe you never heard Mom breathe

Through the walls of the master bedroom—the mirror

Surely dark—scared, I wanted to crawl through the floor

But I was still. Quiet came in time.

I haven't touched a shard yet—I'm wasting time—

I will have to face them so I can go to bed.

When I took another look, refracted face in the floor,

I remembered wives' tales—seven years' bad luck –

And hairlines, webbing in the mirror,

Entangled me— I had to catch my breath.

I won't come close enough to reflect breath. I breathe

Invisible as the past. I finally took the time

To rearrange the room, didn't notice the mirror

Wobbled till it fell—it's a wonder the bed

Isn't scattered full of glass blades, but luck

Pulled it flat as a smashed spider, splayed across the floor.

I can't think of Mom without picturing the floor.

Can you see Dad's face? How we learned to breathe

In the tension, when we thought we lived by luck

And wit. Their tempers tortured time

And vague fears stalked us, as if Dad were in our beds,

Though he wasn't, and Mom wasn't in the mirror.

I'll clear the floor of glass in my own good time,

Calm my thread of breath, then crawl into bed

And weave, if I'm lucky, dreams without mirrors.

For Gram: the Morning after the Dream

Martha Elizabeth Hamilton Sanford, 1904-1984

I.

I dreamt last night I carried you upstairs,

Poured your eggnog and whiskey for the morning,

Got it right, so you didn't stump

Over to slosh more liquor in,

As you did sometimes in life.

II.

We heard of your mythic accidents,

The crippling slip on the ice and the steel

Pin in your hip, which shriveled it,

So you wore one five-inch heel—

We heard of your sudden sprawl

With a bag of birdseed

On icy steps, a new broken hip—

For hours, on your elbows, you shivered,

Waiting to be saved.

You lay near a knotted apple tree

Whose fruit had frozen hard

In the crab grass.

III.

Years you lived half-welcome

In your daughter's crowded home.

Mom pleaded with you to eat.

Once you whacked Dad with your crutch.

Three drunks in the house kept us under siege.

Sometimes I lay beside you

On the hospital bed you bought.

You told how, as a girl, you wound

Braids around your head.

You spoke of the farm or the forty years

You taught mathematics. Usually

I came to you for candy

Or money—for pay

I manicured and pedicured,

Learned to pluck your whiskers.

I cleaned your room, I knew

How alone in a full house and blue

Silk bed-jacket, you cried,

Crumpled tissues,

Sucked butterscotch.

IV.

For high school recreation,

I took your Darvon, Demerol.

V.

Last night I held you as I never had

In life—shadow mother, sick old crone—

I carried you upstairs in too-bright sun,

Poured your eggnog and whiskey,

You nodded to me. I took mine neat,

Felt it light my lips and tongue,

Then woke to darkness,

And a taste of ghost whiskey.

Photo Removed from the Frame

Of all the shots he could have brass-framed

To give us after she died, why

That one with the can

Casually tipped in his hand?

An average lovey-dovey shot of a couple

In the sixties, matching muumuu and aloha shirt,

Having cocktails at the O-club,

A red-and-white beer can between them

In sharp relief like a neon sign,

A valentine. And Mom's high cheekbones

Clean-cut as the clothes she sewed.

She leans over Dad's shoulder.

Handsome as Elvis, his drooped lids

And clamped cigar don't show

The mean streak that hit him when

He drank too much, like the time

He asked me if I ever saw him hit her,

Menace in his eyes. No, I replied, hating him

For my lie. The night she died

Rosie said, *Remember the time*

He poured a whole beer over her head?

Till then I'd blocked the memory,

How he'd glared around the table, challenged

Any kid to rise or yelp or just scrape teeth

Against a fork. *O please*, Mom cried,

Her hair dripping beer, *Please don't.*

Scared sick, we watched and chewed

Our prime rib, went on like no big deal.

Dear Torso, Stone-carved:

Are you still there on his porch, smooth-bellied and gleaming in the corner? He remarked often that you were my torso, your lilting breasts my breasts – but how could that be? You're too heavy to lift, legless and armless as a quadriplegic, headless as a corpse. No voice can emerge from your truncated stub of a neck. Your curvaceous stone reaches down past the contours of your taut belly and elegant navel, down to your sensual tufting, suggesting indentation, labial lines, though your vulva's unseen. Of course you see nothing, eyeless as you are, can't tell that only these pleasing parts, your breasts and sex, are whole, everything else truncated. It always caused me drag that he didn't honor you with a solid stand, a table or even a cinderblock underneath – the least one might do for one so amputated, whose undeniable beauty sunk just below dick-level, a veritable bonsai next to his strapping six feet six. But I never said – didn't speak up on your faceless behalf – why was that? Or am I misremembering now after the centuries since you first appeared? In fact perhaps I asked early on, repeatedly, about his plans to place something beneath you, something simple and stable, not a pedestal for Pete's sake, and he said I just complained, called me a nag. He could be so insulting and angry, sometimes scary. If you had a tongue you might ask, how did the porn creep in? It started with a Valentine or two, then videos. Previous girlfriends loved it, he said. Was I to be a prude? I didn't say early on that I could see chafing on the actors' skin, my eyesight better than his, or that I'd read disturbing reports about the industry filled with runaways. Turned out he had a closet full of DVDs, some he proudly declared "female-friendly." He queued up his favorite scenes so that they exploded onto the screen as soon as I entered his apartment, and then he expected me to perform. So awkward! Then I felt like I'd be a hypocrite to speak up and change course. I worried he'd dump me. Good grief. Sure, we had chemistry, but in hindsight I see how his rock stardom and smooth tongue made me dumb. Mom used to say, "You can't be a rug if you don't lie down." Regrets abound, dear Torso. I wonder now, given climate change, sea level rise, and such a bitter winter: are you still out there so vulnerable, as if struggling for a little dignity? If I had it to do over I'd figure some way to smuggle you away when he wasn't paying attention, which of course is most of the time. I'd give you shelter, do my best at love and respect. But it's too late – I'll just have to do better by other sisters in the future.

Sincerely,

His Ancient, Recent Romance

You

Are not forgiven, your erection

Notwithstanding, from the start I saw

Your slipperiness, lawless direction.

Yet I let myself follow suggestion,

Naively overlooked your glaring flaws,

Thought them charming. Your eager erection

Your signature, an easy distraction

From tawdriness, your unwashed lawless paws

Redirected all my sound direction.

And yes, it's true I can dig erections

And love as if devotion was a flaw

And amplify your value, reflections,

Of gender bias. Such re-direction

Of life energy, intent, plus the draw

Of poetry informed my genuflection.

Your aging and inconstant confection

Offends like a slick dick inside my craw:

You predate, pursue women, perfection

Of your problem, persistent erection.

Wholly Humorless

(with a Salute to Jamaica Kincaid)

So I'm the just-doesn't-get-it girl, the where's-your-sense-of-humor girl,

The oh-come-on-it's-all-in-fun, grimacing girl grown tired. Oh I'm

The ready-to-dress-up girl, the let-me-try-to-please-you girl, the why-

Don't-you-just-chill-out, relax girl, get over it. Oh yes, it's me

Saying sure, whatever you want, the rollover-picking-up-interest girl,

The way-older-than-girl-age-girl, the seasoned, long-tried one,

Borne down on.

       Who can say how many come-ons ignored, let pass? And

How many taken up, girl, who's to say slut? Who cares? Who's to pay

Attention to the legacies of girls? Who to stock the canon? The stockyards

With girls? Who watches MTV and roils with crotching girls? Who

Turns it on? Who turns away? Who draws the line? Who calls it quits?

Who's Girl enough to brave the tough un-girlish world? Maybe only

the wholly humorless, braced I-can-do-it girls aiming to face survival,

Tubman-safe.

Grace Sherwood, Witch of Pungo, Advanced in Age

Indeed they called me a beauty—not that you'd see a trace

at my age, but in all my days I never had a wart,

neither

did I keep it secret I could find receipts for cures—

some teas of roots and herbs—

rosemary, willow-root, ginger,

mint—too many to name, heaven knows. And I had liked

to entertain, and to talk, whatever the topic of the day—

a quality

unbecoming to my sex, some still like to say, but I

had rather be tied than hold my tongue when wronged and then

it was one thing after another—

Any spot could be mark of the Devil, they said,

and despite my once fair face I admit divers moles and

childhood scars—

as when they stripped me, they saw:

spider veins, webbed toes, the palest pink skin:

Mama had called me

              her little pig.

So when they hog-tied and tossed me into water,

well, I declare, the sky went dark almost as pitch and every soul

grew quiet. Now it's called Witch Duck Point, where that crowd

just cheered me on to drown—

              yet I knew the wet hemp

would loosen, and I surfaced.

              Despite the eight years'

hardship in their cell, I found a few kindly souls to call friends,

and outlived most of them who said I kilt their cows

and hogs.   I curst them.   I learnt a few spells.

A Latent Funereal Wail

I'm glad my parents are both dead,

My patriot parents, my veteran parents,

My believing in the possibility of America parents,

My grandchildren of immigrant parents,

My "you-can-be-anything-you-want-to-be" parents,

My had-their-own-faults for sure and finally divorced parents,

My broken, hopeful, Puritan-work-ethic parents,

The beautiful Kathleen and handsome Raymond,

I'm glad they're not here to hear the bluster

Of Donald Trump and his terrifying crusade

Against immigrants, against honesty, against Mexico

Against Muslims, against LBGTQ, against America:

I'm glad my parents died and can't hear

The bluster and insult and degradation

Of the White House hawking cheap dresses and shoes,

I'm glad my dead parents can't hear this dross,

This baloney, bullshit, shit-on-a-shingle, as they would say,

What they suffered and fought for twisted further,

O God, may my dead parents be spared

From the cynical appointments, the lowdown dirty,

May their spirits, their ghosts have no knowledge

Of the Godawful developments of treasonous Trump,

O heavens, how could I not give thanks

That I have no parents, no progenitors, no wise ones

To lean on, to help me navigate, negotiate, resist

The blatant defense of pussy-grabbing, the Predator-in-Chief

Golfing at his Spanish-named resort, spewing tweets—

O my uniformed, "She's a Grand Ole Flag" singing parents,

My road-tripping-across-America-with-five-kids-

Under-the-age-of-eight-and-playing-car-Bingo parents,

My "education-is-the-key-to-success" parents

Are dead, they're dead and gone from this changing earth,

This recurrently flooded coastline, these rising seas:

They both died young, they died by surprise, and so

They never even knew we had a black president,

They don't know about Antarctica's colossal calving

Or the new EPA director being a chemical man,

Or the new Secretary of Education being a hater,

Or the new cabinet being a bastion of billionaires,

Or all the gated places the Trumpish mobsters hail from,

Or the pucker-mouthed, bankrupted swindler

Who's now called commander-in-chief, who hustles hate

From a small island once inhabited by brown people,

O all the innocence lost, the DACAs, the rivers and forests,

My parents are dead and I grieve, I grieve, I grieve.

Universe: Alter-Egos

A Meditation on Strange Attractors

1. Shapes and Sounds

Here a windpipe down to a fiery core,

A churning liquid voice of burst star parts, iron ore

And lava hot can call a game—

Here a song of methane

Rises up from swamp scooped out and stuffed

With refuse cultures scattered over crust—

Somewhere cranky continents shift deep—

Rear their bony limbs in buxom seas—

And seven seas, profane and holy,

Rise and fall like air in an ancient atmosphere—

Here a crawling voice of a globe drones clear

Under a din of light and smoke,

Atoms and hearts, purring star parts—

Old matter, ancient species—

Particles infused with energy,

Water and sunlight, periodic chemistry.

Hear the groan of so many souls, centuries old,

Who bathe and bake under a ball

Of burning time, who bask

Anonymous as kin on Thanksgiving—

Listen: lean both ears:

Windy rhythms pour through leaves

Green or crackling,

And ripple rivers and streams

Content as cats or humming

Traffic below city windows

Sucking and spewing exhaust.

Hear the near voices still plants seem to breathe—

Above the surface of this sphere, a sonorous blur

Spins and speeds.

2. Dreams

In a mind's eye, in a metal mirror, I see

How I carry my home in my head

And crawl along a crust

Of a small sphere in a minor galaxy—

And ever matter presses me

Warmly awake in the dark:

In rippling water, I see

A bent body, tall weeds,

Rainbow oils glistening—

Around me pavement leads

Bunches of bustling lives

Under hazy skies.

A seawall laps black brown,

A sign reads "No Fishing,"

And a rat as long as my right foot

Almost gets squashed in my stride.

The rat's sunken black

Eyes buzz with flies

But its tail arcs in air

Like a paisley design.

Once I stared at a glaring screen

And saw those sand-piles slipping

Off barges tugs push down polluted

Rivers were souls, ashen and common—

My sight dims, dependent on this tapered

Arm of a minor galaxy.

3. You

Close your face in hands and feel your bone

Beneath enfolding membrane—

Sometimes feel your hip sockets

Unlocking femurs in runs or jumps—

Feel your cord stiffen in tight spots

And jaws lock

Inside the muscles of your mask—

Feel your body beneath, inside, a frame and core, a plane—

How matter makes you

Atoms and energy

Burning and being in a mind's eye

While yawning jaw swings wide

And lips withdraw to teeth, gums, glistening tongue—

Magic muscle in this small country.

Feel your throat steer warm breath free

Without asking

And pull random samplings back

Into what seems a battery-

Operated organism, half perhaps

A life yet charged—

Feel how womb tightens—

Feel heart and bowels,

Stomach churning meat or greens—

Feel the weight of the form you carry—

Milagro-machine more sure than you,

Your part and parcel—

Feel your iron rivers pulsing,

As your airways breathe like trees,

Unconsciously.

4. Strange Attractors

Strange attractors puzzle me:

Weather patterns and EEGs

Conjuring cool art on computer screens—

Peeling petals, rippling seeds—

Original as chaos

Kicked up and settled as mythologies

Or the studies or sediment and stone.

How matter grows fat and hungry,

Licks and tastes new alchemies—

Glowing sludge and factories'

Corpses sunk in salty stews

Of everlasting opportunities

To be atoms, energy

Supple and crusty

As roots, reptiles, continents' caves—

Passageways

To the core of a small orb

Whose layers bake like pastries,

Even as heat

Sun sheds on dusty prairies—

My dry skin flakes like silicon

Sifted on the growing heap—

My taste-buds bloom as I eat

And water and wind suck and seal me

In light years, chaos, chemistry—

Atoms, energy

Dapple spidery galaxies

And edges of minor minds.

Born on Naval Base Corpus Christi, Texas, USA, Renée Ellen Olander grew up on and around military bases in Massachusetts, Michigan, Hawai'i, and Southeastern Virginia. A longtime caregiver, Olander studied at Mary Baldwin U., Old Dominion U., and the U. of Southern Maine. She has taught at university, K-12 and community levels for more than 30 years, and she often walks in the woods.

CPSIA information can be obtained
at www.ICGtesting.com
Printed in the USA
FSHW01n0527180818
51373FS